super simple quilts #4

with ALEX ANDERSON & LIZ ANELOSKI

9 Appliqué Projects to Sew With or Without a Machine

C&T PUBLISHING

Text copyright © 2009 by Alex Anderson and Liz Aneloski

Artwork copyright © 2009 by C&T Publishing, Inc.

Publisher: Amy Marson

Creative Director: Gailen Runge

Editors: Liz Aneloski and Cynthia Bix

Technical Editors: Carolyn Aune and Ellen Pahl

Copyeditor/Proofreader: Wordfirm Inc.

Design Director: Christina Jarumay

Cover/Book Designer: Kerry Graham

Production Coordinator: Casey Dukes

Production Editor: Alice Mace Nakanishi

Illustrator: Tim Manibusan

Photography by Christina McCarty Francis and Diane
Pedersen of C&T Publishing unless otherwise noted

Published by C&T Publishing, Inc., P.O. Box 1456,
Lafayette, CA 94549

contents

acknowledgments

We'd like to thank the following companies for providing
the wonderful products used in the quilts:

Dill Buttons

FreeSpirit Fabrics

Westminster Fabrics

Timeless Treasures
Fabrics

RJR Fabrics

Robert Kaufman Fabrics

Warm Company for
Lite Steam-A-Seam 2

Quilters Dream Batting

Presencia Threads

introduction

These quilts can be first quilts for beginners or fast quilts for more experienced quilters looking for the perfect gift, donation, or baby quilt. Choose from three raw-edge appliqué techniques:

No handwork required (all machine appliqué)

No machine required (all hand appliqué)

Mix & match the hand and machine methods for your perfect style

This book offers

3 quilt designs using

3 raw-edge appliqué styles in

3 sizes with

3 binding techniques

Choose the size of quilt you want, and from one materials list you can make any of the three quilt designs. This means you can choose a size, shop for fabric (photos of fabric swatches will help you), and then go home and decide which quilt design you want to make. Choose an appliqué style (appliqué and quilt in one step) and binding technique, and you're done! See how easy?

We have included basic guidance to get you started and a great list of books (page 27) you can refer to if you want more information.

I often have the pleasure of brainstorming with Liz. I always treasure the time together. We each bring our own perspective to the table, and more often than not, we are keenly in sync. One such occasion was in the recent past. We were chatting about what sort of book was needed. As usual, life took its twists and turns, and that conversation was left on the back burner, or so I thought. Several months later I received a call from Liz, and she wanted to show me "something." Bingo, her quilts hit the nail on the head. She asked if I would be interested in providing the general quiltmaking instructions for the book and before we knew it, Liz and I were co-authors! We are both very excited about this collaboration— fast, fun, simple projects, perfect for the beginner or the seasoned quilter who wants a quick project, in perfect C&T style.

—Alex

Over the many years that Alex and I have known each other, our relationship has developed through many different experiences: quilt show chair and vendor, quilting friends/parents, editor and author, and now co-authors. The fun just never ends. With this book, we have combined Alex's expertise in quiltmaking knowledge with my design and project writing skills. I hope you have fun with the simple designs, techniques, and many options that await you.

—Liz

the basics

 See page 27 for sources of more detailed information.

essential supplies

■ Sewing machine (good working condition, with proper tension [refer to the manufacturer's guide for proper adjustment], an even stitch, and a good-quality size 80 needle)

■ 45mm rotary cutter

Straight-edge cutter

Decorative-edge cutters

■ 18" × 24" self-healing rotary cutting mat (must be used with the rotary cutter)

■ 6" × 12" rotary cutting ruler

■ Scissors (small, for cutting threads)

■ Pins (thin, fine quilter's or silk pins work best)

■ Sewing thread (good-quality matching or neutral-color cotton)

■ Seam ripper (sharp, good quality)

■ Iron

■ Safety pins (1" long for basting)

■ Perle cotton or crochet cotton thread (for tying and big-stitch hand quilting)

Presencia perle cotton

■ Needles (darning or chenille needles with eyes large enough for the perle cotton for tying and big-stitch hand quilting)

■ Buttons

rotary cutting

■ Practice and learn to use the rotary cutter safely and properly.

■ Always close the safety latch or replace the cover on the rotary cutter after each cut.

■ Always cut away from your body, at a 90° angle.

■ Hold the rotary cutter as shown, with your index finger extended along the back of the cutter.

Left-handed

Right-handed

■ Place the side of the rotary cutter blade directly against the edge of the ruler.

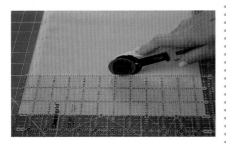

Place the blade against the edge of the ruler.

1. Fold the fabric selvage (finished edge) to selvage, then fold again.

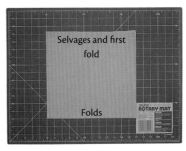

Fold the fabric twice.

2. Align a vertical line of the ruler with the bottom fold of the fabric. Trim to straighten and square up the raw edges.

Left-handed   Right-handed

3. Line up the vertical measurement on the ruler with the trimmed edge of the fabric. Cut the size and number of strips indicated in the charts included with the instructions for each project.

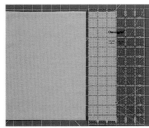
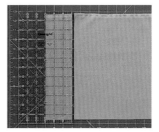

Left-handed   Right-handed

4. Rotate the mat and fabric. Trim off the uneven raw edges to square up the short edges. Line up the measurement on the ruler with the trimmed edge of the fabric. Cut the size and number of units (squares and rectangles) indicated in the charts included with the instructions for each project.

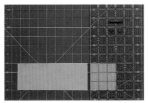
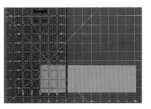

Left-handed   Right-handed

fusing

The fusing method used for the quilts in this book is a little different than you might usually use. Please read the directions before proceeding.

1. With a straight-edge rotary cutting blade, cut the pieces from paper-backed fusible adhesive using the second chart in each project.

2. Remove the paper backing and fuse the pieces to the appropriate fabrics, ½" apart, using the third chart in each project.

3. With the wavy-edge rotary cutting blade, cut out the pieces, leaving ¼" of unfused fabric around the edges of the fusible adhesive. This will allow you to stitch through the fabric only, not through the fusible adhesive. Don't worry if your cutting isn't perfect, it doesn't matter.

layering the quilt

BATTING AND BACKING

Batting (low-loft polyester or cotton, approximately 2" larger than the quilt top on each side)

Backing (approximately 2" larger than the quilt top on each side)

If your quilt top is larger than one width of fabric, you will need to sew pieces of fabric together to make the backing (trim off the selvages first). If you're using leftover fabrics, sew pieces together to achieve the size listed in the Materials chart. You may have some leftover fabrics from making the project quilts to use for backing and binding.

LAYERING

1. Place the backing wrong side up. Secure the backing to a large, flat surface, pulling the backing smooth and taut (not too tight). Use masking tape to secure on a table or hard floor or T-pins on nonloop carpet.

2. Place the batting on top of the backing and smooth out the wrinkles.

3. Smooth the quilt top onto the batting, right side up.

BASTING

Pin baste evenly across the quilt about every 3" with safety pins.

appliqué and quilt in one step

After layering and basting, quilt through all three layers to secure the appliqué pieces.

METHOD #1: MACHINE APPLIQUÉ AND QUILTING (NO HANDWORK REQUIRED)

This is a simple method of machine quilting to get you started. Machine quilting takes practice.

> **note** The larger the quilt, the more challenging it is to machine quilt.

■ You must use a walking/even-feed foot on your sewing machine for the layers to feed through the machine evenly.

■ Refer to the sewing machine manufacturer's instructions for thread tension guidance. Sew on a test piece of layered fabric, batting, and backing until you achieve the perfect thread tension.

■ Begin and end the lines of stitching using very tiny stitches.

■ Use a slightly longer stitch than you use for piecing.

■ Machine quilt lines of stitches ⅛" inside the edges of the appliqué pieces, starting from the center of the quilt and working out. Then, add extra quilting in the background areas, as needed.

METHOD #2: BIG-STITCH HAND APPLIQUÉ AND QUILTING (NO MACHINE REQUIRED)

This method is not recommended for quilts that will be heavily used, because this style of hand quilting does not give maximum stability. It is best used for wallhangings.

1. Knot one end of the thread. (The quilts in this book were quilted with Presencia perle cotton or crochet cotton thread.)

2. Insert the needle from the back of the quilt and pull the thread through to the front, leaving the knot showing on the back. Sew a running stitch, making the stitches approximately ¼″ long, ⅛″ inside from the edges of the appliqué pieces. Then, add extra quilting in the background areas, if needed.

Running stitch

3. When you come to the end of the stitching or have approximately 6″ of thread left, knot the thread on the back of the quilt as shown below.

A Take a tiny stitch through just the backing and batting.

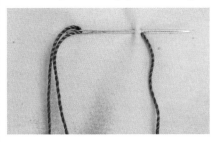

Left-handed Right-handed

B Put the needle through the loop. **C** Pull it tight.

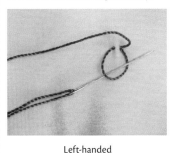 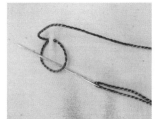

Left-handed Right-handed

D Run the needle through the backing and batting about ½″.

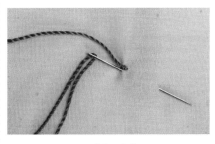 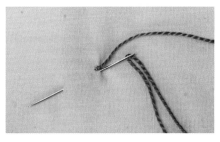

Left-handed Right-handed

E Trim off the thread where it exits the batting.

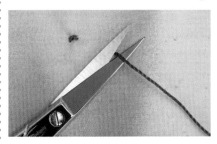 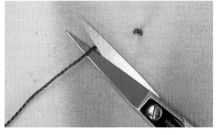

Left-handed Right-handed

tying

Tying is another option for securing the quilt layers and is an alternative to machine appliqué and quilting (page 6) and big-stitch hand appliqué and quilting (pages 6–7).

1. Decide whether you want the knots and tails to be on the front or the back of the quilt.

2. Thread a large-eyed needle with the tying thread. (The quilts in this book were tied with DMC perle cotton or crochet cotton thread.)

note You can use a single or double thread, depending on how much you want the thread to show.

3. Push the needle through all 3 layers, so it comes out through the other side.

note If you want the knots on the front, push the needle in from the front. If you want the knots on the back, push the needle in from the back.

4. Push the needle back through the layers, approximately ⅛″–¼″ from where it originally went through the layers. Pull the thread, leaving a 1½″–2″ tail.

5. Tie the knot as shown to the right. This knot is more secure than a square knot. Trim the thread ends to the length you want.

A Tie a half-knot.

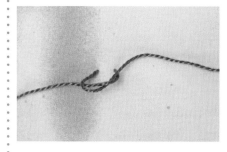

B Pull it tight.

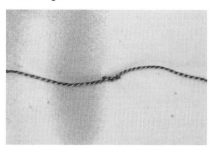

C Hold the 2 strands and the needle as shown.

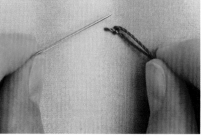

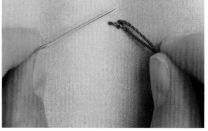

Left-handed   Right-handed

D Take the needle around the threads. Then, pull the needle through the loops.

Left-handed   Right-handed

E Let go of the thread end that is attached to the needle and hold only the short thread tail in your other hand.

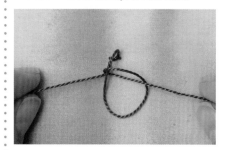

F Pull the knot tight

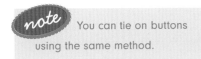

note You can tie on buttons using the same method.

binding

We recommend that you use leftover fabrics for binding and then supplement as necessary. You can use one to four different fabrics. Look at the quilts throughout the book for ideas.

BINDING METHOD #1
(NO HANDWORK REQUIRED)

1. Follow Steps 1–4 for Binding Method #3, pages 10–11.

2. Align the raw edges of the binding with the top edge of the back of the quilt. Let the binding extend ½" past the corners of the quilt. Sew using a ¼" seam allowance. Repeat for the bottom edge of the quilt.

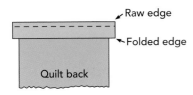

Sew the binding to the top edge of the quilt.

3. Flip the finished edge of the binding over the raw edge of the quilt and machine stitch to the front of the quilt using straight or decorative stitches. Trim the ends even with the edge of the quilt.

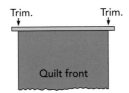

Fold the binding to the front, stitch, and trim.

4. Measure the quilt length through the middle from top to bottom. Trim 2 binding strips the length of the quilt plus 1". Fold and press. Align and sew the strips to the back of the quilt as in Step 2, leaving ½" of binding past the corners. Fold over the ends of the binding to create a finished edge before folding the binding to the front of the quilt. Machine stitch to the front of the quilt, as in Step 3.

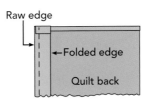

Fold the ends and stitch the side binding to the front.

BINDING METHOD #2
(NO MACHINE REQUIRED)

1. Trim the batting and backing even with the edges of the quilt top.

2. For the wallhanging/crib size project quilts, cut 4 strips 3½" × width of fabric. Skip Step 3. For twin- and queen-size project quilts, cut as many 2¼"-wide strips as you need to go all the way around the quilt, plus 10" or more extra.

3. Sew the strips together using diagonal seams to make 4 lengths at least 2" longer than the edges of the quilt.

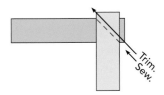

Piece the strips using diagonal seams. Trim.

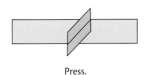

Press.

4. Measure the quilt width through the middle from side to side. Trim 2 binding strips the width of the quilt plus 1".

5. Fold the strips lengthwise, wrong sides together, with one long edge ¼" from the other long edge, and press.

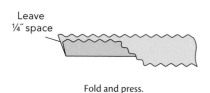

Leave ¼" space

Fold and press.

6. Fold in half lengthwise, placing the folded edge even with the wavy edge.

7. Insert the top edge of the quilt into the fold created in Step 6 with the raw edges of the binding on the front side of the quilt. Let the binding extend ½" past the corners of the quilt. Hand sew through all layers using the big-stitch method (pages 6–7). Repeat for the bottom edge.

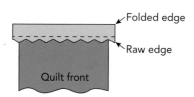

Folded edge

Raw edge

Quilt front

Sew the binding to the top and bottom edges of the quilt.

8. Trim the ends even with the corners of the quilt.

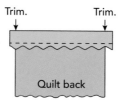

Trim. Trim.

Quilt back

Fold the binding to the back, stitch, and trim.

9. Measure the quilt length through the middle from top to bottom. Trim 2 binding strips the length of the quilt plus 1". Fold and press. Align and sew the strips as before, leaving ½" of the binding past the corners. Fold over the ends of the binding to create a finished edge before folding the binding to the back of the quilt. Hand slipstitch the binding, including the ends, in place.

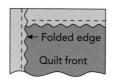

Folded edge

Quilt front

Fold the ends and stitch the side binding.

BINDING METHOD #3
(MACHINE AND HAND)

1. Trim the batting and backing even with the edges of the quilt top.

2. Cut as many 2¼"-wide strips as you need to go all the way around the quilt, plus 10" or more extra.

3. Sew the strips together using diagonal seams to make one long length.

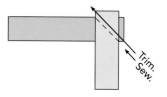

Trim.
Sew.

Piece the strips using diagonal seams. Trim.

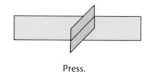

Press.

4. Fold the strips in half lengthwise, wrong sides together, and press.

Fold and press.

5. With the raw edges of the quilt and binding aligned, pin the binding to the front of the quilt, beginning a few inches from a corner, leaving the first 6" of the binding unattached. Start sewing using a ¼" seam allowance.

6. Stop ¼" from the first corner of the quilt and backstitch one stitch.

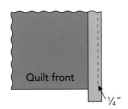

Stitch ¼" from a corner.

7. Lift the presser foot and needle. Rotate the quilt one-quarter turn. Fold the binding at a right angle so it extends straight above the quilt.

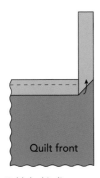

Fold the binding up.

8. Bring the binding down, even with the edge of the quilt. Begin sewing again at the folded edge, stopping ¼" from the next corner and backstitching one stitch.

Fold down and stitch.

9. Repeat Steps 6–8 for all the sides of the quilt. Stop sewing 6" from where you started.

10. Overlap the tails and trim, leaving a 2" overlap.

11. Turn under the beginning tail end ¼".

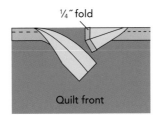

Turn under the end ¼".

12. Place the ending tail end inside the beginning tail end.

Place the ending tail inside the beginning tail.

13. Adjust the binding length, pin, and sew to finish the seam.

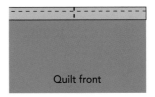

Pin, then sew.

14. Fold to the back of the quilt and hand stitch to finish.

Fold to the back and stitch.

almost woven

Almost Woven (all hand) by Liz Aneloski

Wall/Crib: 40″ × 40″

Twin: 63″ × 87″

Queen: 84″ × 92″

materials

Yardages are based on 42″-wide fabric.

Fabric	Wall/Crib	Twin	Queen
Fabric #1	1¼ yards	3⅞ yards	5¼ yards
Fabric #2	⅜ yard	¾ yard	1 yard
Fabric #3	¾ yard	2¼ yards	3½ yards
Fabric #4	½ yard	1¼ yards	1⅝ yards
Fabric #5	½ yard	¾ yard	1 yard
Fabric #6	¾ yard	1½ yards	2¼ yards
Paper-backed fusible adhesive (based on 12″ width)	2 yards	5½ yards	6¼ yards
Backing	44″ × 44″ (Use leftovers and supplement as necessary.)	67″ × 91″ (Use leftovers and supplement as necessary.)	88″ × 96″ (Use leftovers and supplement as necessary.)
Binding	Leftovers or ⅝ yard	Leftovers or 1 yard	Leftovers or 1⅛ yards
Batting	44″ × 44″	67″ × 91″	88″ × 96″

cutting

Fabric	Wall/Crib		Twin		Queen	
	Number of Strips*	Size of Pieces	Number of Strips*	Size of Pieces	Number of Strips*	Size of Pieces
Fusible Adhesive	4	½″ × 22½″	5	½″ × 36″	5	½″ × 52½″*
			3	½″ × 59½″*	5	½″ × 60″*
	4	1″ × 22½″	5	1″ × 36″	5	1″ × 52½″*
			3	1″ × 59½″*	5	1″ × 60″*
	6	1½″ × 22½″	9	1½″ × 36″	9	1½″ × 52½″*
			5	1½″ × 59½″*	7	1½″ × 60″*
	4 (inner borders)	½″ × 33½″	2 (inner borders)	½″ × 52½″*	2 (inner borders)	½″ × 69½″*
			2 (inner borders)	½″ × 76½″*	2 (inner borders)	½″ × 77½″*
	4 (outer borders)	½″ × 39½″	2 (outer borders)	½″ × 62½″*	2 (outer borders)	½″ × 83½″*
			2 (outer borders)	½″ × 86½″*	2 (outer borders)	½″ × 91½″*
#3 Inner Border	4	3″ × 34″	2	5½″ × 53″**	2	6″ × 70″**
			2	5½″ × 77″**	2	6″ × 78″**
#6 Outer Border	4	4″ × 40″	2	6″ × 63″**	2	8″ × 84″**
			2	6″ × 87″**	2	8″ × 92″**
#1 Background	1	30″ × 30″	1	44″ × 68″***	1	60″ × 68″***

* Cut strips and fuse multiple pieces, end to end, on the fabric to create the lengths indicated. ** Cut strips the width of the fabric, sew together into one long strip, and then cut the lengths indicated. *** Cut pieces of fabric, and sew them together to make the size needed.

preparation

CENTER STRIPS

1. Using a straight-edge rotary cutter, cut out the fusible adhesive strips as directed in the cutting chart (page 13).

2. Referring to the chart below, place the fusible adhesive strips for the quilt center (not the ones designated for the borders) ½" apart and at least ½" from all raw edges, on the wrong side of the appropriate fabrics. Fuse following the manufacturer's instructions.

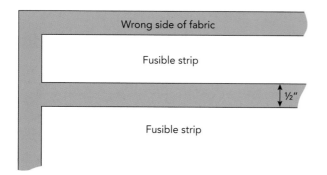

Place fusible adhesive strips on appropriate fabrics ½" apart.

3. Using a wavy-edge rotary cutter, cut down the center of the ½" spaces and around all edges of the strips, leaving ¼" of unfused fabric around the edges of the fusible adhesive. This will allow you to stitch through the fabric only, not through the fusible adhesive. Don't worry if your cutting isn't perfect; it doesn't matter.

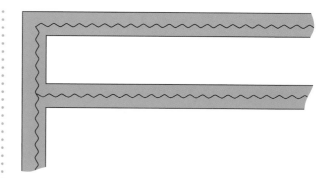

Cut down center of ½" spaces and ¼" from other edges.

BORDER STRIPS

1. Using the wavy-edge rotary cutting blade, cut out the inner and outer border strips as directed in the cutting chart.

2. Using the ½" fusible adhesive strips designated for the borders, fuse the adhesive strips to the wrong side of the border strips ⅜" from one long wavy edge.

Place fusible adhesive on border strips.

3. Mark the center of each border strip and the center of each side of the background piece with a pin.

Fabric	Wall/Crib Fusible Strip Width	Number of Strips	Twin Fusible Strip Width	Number of Strips	Queen Fusible Strip Width	Number of Strips
Fabric #2	½"	1	½"	2	½"	2
			1"	1	1"	1
	1½"	2	1½"	4	1½"	5
Fabric #3	½"	1	½"	2	½"	3
	1"	2	1"	2	1"	2
			1½"	2	1½"	2
Fabric #4	½"	1	½"	2	½"	2
	1"	1	1"	2	1"	4
	1½"	2	1½"	4	1½"	5
Fabric #5	½"	1	½"	2	½"	3
	1"	1	1"	3	1"	3
	1½"	2	1½"	4	1½"	4

construction

1. Match the marked centers and fuse the inner borders to the background; add the side borders first, then the top and bottom borders. The wavy edge of the inner border should overlap the background by 1" for the wall/crib quilt, so for the wall/crib quilt 28" × 28" of background fabric remains showing. The ends of the borders will overlap.

2. Referring to the quilt construction diagram, arrange the center strips approximately 1½" apart. Place the horizontal strips first, about 3" from the top and bottom, and then the vertical strips, about 2¾" from the sides. Fuse to the background.

3. Fuse the outer border to the inner border, overlapping it by 1"; add the side borders first, then the top and bottom borders, overlapping the ends.

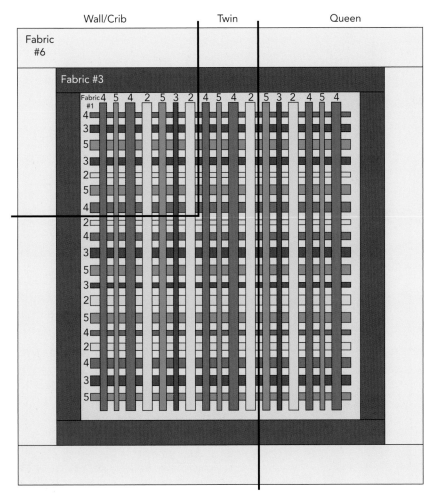

Quilt construction

finishing

1. Layer and baste the quilt (page 6).

2. Stitch around all of the appliqué strips, ⅛" inside all of the wavy edges (pages 6–7).* Stitch around the inner and outer borders ⅛" from the edges. Then, stitch around the strips that form the top layer of strips ⅛" from the edges. Stitch ⅛" from the short ends of the strips that form the bottom layer.

3. If more quilting is needed, choose a method to secure the layers (pages 6–9).

4. Trim to square up the quilt, and choose a binding technique (pages 9–11).

For the all-by-machine method (No Handwork Required), machine stitch using a slightly longer than normal stitch length.

For the all-by-hand method (No Machine Required), hand stitch using running stitches (page 7) with perle cotton thread.

For the combination method (Machine and Hand), mix and match the machine and hand techniques, as desired.

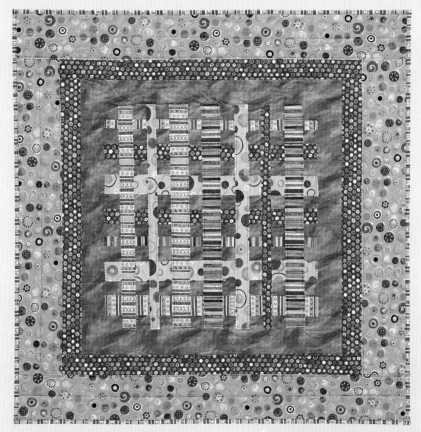

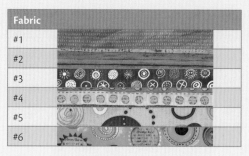

Fabric	
#1	
#2	
#3	
#4	
#5	
#6	

Almost Woven (all machine) by Liz Aneloski

Fabric	
#1	
#2	
#3	
#4	
#5	
#6	

Almost Woven (hand and machine) by Liz Aneloski

divided circle in a square

Divided Circle in a Square (hand and machine) by Liz Aneloski

Wall/Crib: 32″ × 42″

Twin: 64″ × 84″

Queen: 84″ × 96″

materials

Yardages are based on 42″-wide fabric.

Fabric		Wall/Crib	Twin	Queen
Fabric #1		1¼ yards	3⅞ yards	5¼ yards
Fabric #2		⅜ yard	¾ yard	1 yard
Fabric #3		¾ yard	2¼ yards	3½ yards
Fabric #4		½ yard	1¼ yards	1⅝ yards
Fabric #5		½ yard	¾ yard	1 yard
Fabric #6		¾ yard	1½ yards	2¼ yards
Paper-backed fusible adhesive (based on 12″ width)		2½ yards	9¾ yards	14 yards
Backing		36″ × 46″ (Use leftovers and supplement as necessary.)	68″ × 88″ (Use leftovers and supplement as necessary.)	88″ × 100″ (Use leftovers and supplement as necessary.)
Binding		Leftovers or ⅝ yard	Leftovers or 1 yard	Leftovers or 1⅛ yards
Batting		36″ × 46″	68″ × 88″	88″ × 100″

cutting

Fabric	Wall/Crib		Twin		Queen	
	Number of Pieces	Size of Pieces	Number of Pieces	Size of Pieces	Number of Pieces	Size of Pieces
Fusible Adhesive	4	8½″ × 8½″*	16	8½″ × 8½″*	24	8½″ × 8½″*
	4	10½″ × 10½″	16	10½″ × 10½″	24	10½″ × 10½″
	2	½″ × 32″ (top & bottom borders)	8	½″ × 32″ (top & bottom borders)	12	½″ × 32″ (side borders)
	2	½″ × 42″ (side borders)	8	½″ × 42″ (side borders)	12	½″ × 42″ (top & bottom borders)
#1 Background	1	24″ × 34″	4	24″ × 34″	6	24″ × 34″
#3 Borders	2	5″ × 32″ (top & bottom borders)	8	5″ × 32″ (top & bottom borders)	12	5″ × 32″ (side borders)
	2	5″ × 42″ (side borders)	8	5″ × 42″ (side borders)	12	5″ × 42″ (top & bottom borders)

* Draw an arc 8½″ from one corner of the square, and cut on the drawn line. Repeat for all drawn pieces.

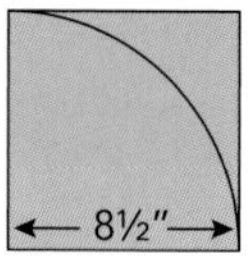

Draw arc 8½″ from corner.

preparation
APPLIQUÉ PIECES

1. Using the straight-edge rotary cutting blade, cut out the fusible adhesive pieces as directed in the cutting chart.

2. Place the fusible adhesive shapes (not the ones marked for the borders) ½" apart on the wrong side of the appropriate fabrics. Fuse following the manufacturer's instructions.

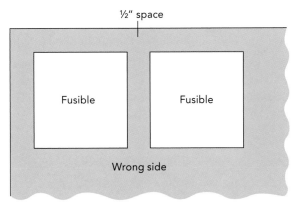

Place fusible pieces ½" apart.

3. Using the wavy-edge rotary cutting blade, cut out the pieces, leaving ¼" of unfused fabric around the edge of the fusible adhesive. This will allow you to stitch through the fabric only, not through the fusible adhesive, creating a softer edge.

Cut out pieces ¼" from edges of fusible adhesive.

Fabric	Wall/Crib		Twin		Queen	
	Fusible Piece	Number of Pieces	Fusible Piece	Number of Pieces	Fusible Piece	Number of Pieces
Fabric #2	¼ circles	2	¼ circles	8	¼ circles	12
Fabric #4	10½" × 10½"	2	10½" × 10½"	8	10½" × 10½"	12
Fabric #5	¼ circles	2	¼ circles	8	¼ circles	12
Fabric #6	10½" × 10½"	2	10½" × 10½"	8	10½" × 10½"	12

BORDER STRIPS

1. Using the wavy-edge rotary cutting blade, cut out the border strips as directed in the chart.

2. Using the ½" fusible adhesive strips marked for the borders, fuse the adhesive strips to the wrong side of the border strips ⅜" from one long wavy edge.

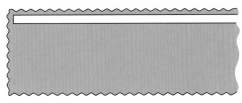

Place fusible adhesive on border strips.

3. Mark the center of each border strip and the center of each side of the background with a pin.

construction

1. Match the marked centers and fuse the borders to the background; add the side borders first, then the top and bottom borders. The border should overlap the background by 1", so 22" × 32" of background fabric remains showing. The ends of the borders will overlap.

2. Position and overlap the squares on the background, creating a larger square. The top points of this square should be on the background, 1" from the border. The side points of this square should be on the side borders, 1" from the outer edge of the quilt top. Fuse to the background.

3. Position and overlap the quarter-circles on the center square from Step 2, creating a circle. The outermost edges of the circle should be 2" from the edges of the square. Fuse to the background.

finishing

1. Layer and baste the quilt (page 6).

2. Stitch around all of the appliqué pieces, ⅛" inside all the wavy edges (pages 6–7).* Stitch around the borders ⅛" from the edges.

3. If more quilting is needed, choose a method to secure the layers (pages 6–9).

4. Trim to square up the quilt, and choose a binding technique (pages 9–11).

For the all-by-machine method (No Handwork Required), machine stitch using a slightly longer than normal stitch length.

For the all-by-hand method (No Machine Required), hand stitch using running stitches (page 7) with perle cotton thread.

For the combination method (Machine and Hand), mix and match the machine and hand techniques, as desired.

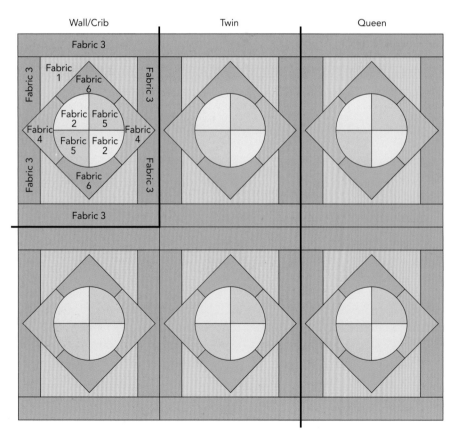

Quilt construction

Divided Circle in a Square (all hand) by Liz Aneloski

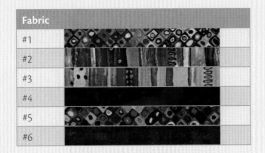

Divided Circle in a Square (hand and machine) by Liz Aneloski

geometric explosion

Geometric Explosion (all machine) by Liz Aneloski

Wall/Crib: 40" × 40"

Twin: 64" × 84"

Queen: 84" × 92"

materials

Yardages are based on 42"-wide fabric.

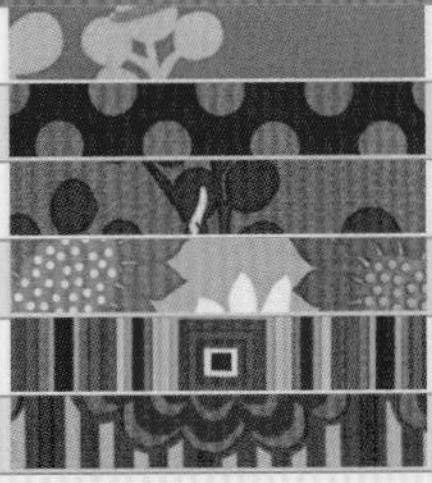

Fabric	Wall/Crib	Twin	Queen
Fabric #1	1¼ yards	3⅞ yards	5¼ yards
Fabric #2	⅜ yard	¾ yard	1 yard
Fabric #3	¾ yard	2¼ yards	3½ yards
Fabric #4	½ yard	1¼ yards	1⅝ yards
Fabric #5	½ yard	¾ yard	1 yard
Fabric #6	¾ yard	1½ yards	2¼ yards
Paper-backed fusible adhesive (based on 12" width)	3 yards	7⅞ yards	9⅞ yards
Backing	44" × 44" (Use leftovers and supplement as necessary.)	68" × 88" (Use leftovers and supplement as necessary.)	88" × 96" (Use leftovers and supplement as necessary.)
Binding	Leftovers or ⅝ yard	Leftovers or 1 yard	Leftovers or 1⅛ yards
Batting	44" × 44"	68" × 88"	88" × 96"

cutting

Fabric	Wall/Crib		Twin		Queen	
	Number of Pieces*	Size of Pieces	Number of Pieces*	Size of Pieces	Number of Pieces*	Size of Pieces
Fusible Adhesive	4 of each	5", 6", 7", 8" circles	4 of each	5", 6", 7", 8", 9" circles	4 of each	5", 6", 7", 8", 9", 10" circles
	4 of each	3", 4", 5" squares	4 of each	3", 4", 5", 6" squares	4 of each	3", 4", 5", 6", 7" squares
			2	7" squares	2	8" squares
	1	16" square*	1	24" square*	1	24" square*
	1	12" circle**	1	18" circle**	1	18" circle**
Fabric #1	1	40" × 40"	1	64" × 84"***	1	84" × 92"***

* Use multiple widths of fusible adhesive as needed.

** To cut a 12" circle, cut a 12" square, fold it in half vertically and
   horizontally, draw an arc 6" from the corner with the folds,
   and cut on the arc line through all 4 layers. For the 18" circle,
   use the same method, using multiple widths of fusible adhesive
   as needed.

*** Cut pieces of fabric, and sew them together to make the size needed.

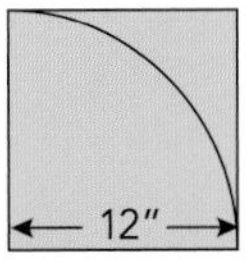

Fold, draw a circle, and cut out.

preparation

APPLIQUÉ PIECES

1. Using the straight-edge rotary cutting blade or scissors, cut out the fusible adhesive pieces as directed in the cutting chart.

2. Place the fusible adhesive shapes ½" apart on the wrong side of the appropriate fabrics. Fuse following the manufacturer's instructions.

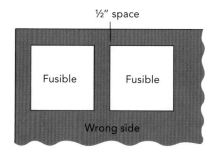

Place fusible adhesive shapes on appropriate fabrics ½" apart.

Fabroc	Wall/Crib		Twin		Queen	
	Fusible Piece	Number of Pieces	Fusible Piece	Number of Pieces	Fusible Piece	Number of Pieces
Fabric #2			9" circles	4	9" circles	4
	6" circles	4	6" circles	4	6" circles	4
			7" squares	2	7" squares	4
	4" squares	4	4" squares	4	4" squares	4
Fabric #3	12" circle	1	18" circle	1	18" circle	1
Fabric #4					10" circles	4
	7" circles	4	7" circles	4	7" circles	4
			6" squares	4	6" squares	4
	3" squares	4	3" squares	4	3" squares	4
Fabric #5			8" circles	4	8" circles	4
	5" circles	4	5" circles	4	5" circles	4
			7" squares	2	8" squares	2
	5" squares	4	5" squares	4	5" squares	4
Fabric #6	16" square	1	24" square	1	24" square	1

3. Using the wavy-edge rotary cutting blade, cut out the appliqué shapes, leaving ¼" of unfused fabric around the edge of the fusible adhesive. This will allow you to stitch through the fabric only, not through the fusible adhesive, and it creates a softer edge.

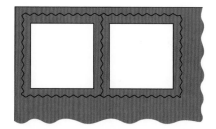

Cut out pieces ¼" from edges of fusible adhesive.

construction

1. Fold the background fabric square in half in both directions, and press. Fold the background fabric square in half diagonally in both directions, and press.

 Fold in half horizontally and vertically, then diagonally in both directions, and press.

2. Finger-press the large center square appliqué diagonally in both directions. Align the square in the exact center of the background fabric where the pressed fold lines intersect, and press to fuse.

3. Finger-press the large center circle in half in both directions. Fuse the circle in the center of the square.

4. Finger-press each square from corner to corner. Align the fold lines on the squares with the fold lines on the background fabric, overlapping as shown, and fuse.

5. Finger-press each circle in half. Align the fold lines on the circles with the fold lines on the background fabric, overlapping as shown, and fuse.

6. Press the quilt top to remove any remaining fold lines.

finishing

1. Layer and baste the quilt (page 6).

2. Stitch around all of the appliqué pieces, ⅛" inside all the wavy edges (pages 6–7).*

3. If more quilting is needed, choose a method to secure the layers (pages 6–9).

4. Trim to square up the quilt, and choose a binding technique (pages 9–11).

For the all-by-machine method (No Handwork Required), machine stitch using a slightly longer than normal stitch length.

For the all-by-hand method (No Machine Required), hand stitch using running stitches (page 7) with perle cotton thread.

For the combination method (Machine and Hand), mix and match the machine and hand techniques, as desired.

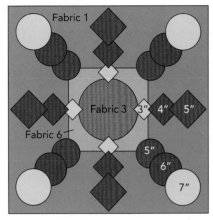

Wall/crib quilt construction

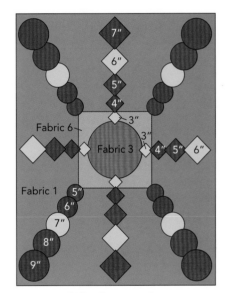

Twin quilt construction

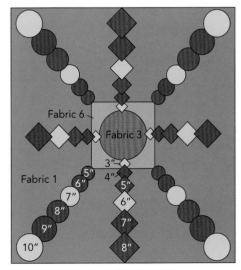

Queen quilt construction

Geometric Explosion (all hand) by Liz Aneloski

Fabric	
#1	
#2	
#3	
#4	
#5	
#6	

Fabric	
#1	
#2	
#3	
#4	
#5	
#6	

Geometric Explosion (hand and machine) by Liz Aneloski